Boston Tea Party

A Hands-On History Look at Events Leading Up to the Revolutionary War Including the Boston Tea Party

Written by Mary Tucker

Illustrated by Judy Hierstein

Teaching & Learning Company

1204 Buchanan St., P.O. Box 10
Carthage, IL 62321-0010

This book belongs to

Cover art by Judy Hierstein

Copyright © 2001, Teaching & Learning Company

ISBN No. 1-57310-302-0

Printing No. 987654321

Teaching & Learning Company
1204 Buchanan St., P.O. Box 10
Carthage, IL 62321-0010

Table of Contents

Dear Teacher or Parent,

Every time we put our hands on our hearts and say the Pledge of Allegiance to the American flag, we are remembering and honoring the history of America, including its colonial beginnings. What caused the American Revolution? What made those million or so people, many of them originally from England, decide that they owed no allegiance to England, but only to America which wasn't even a united country yet? Farmers, lawyers, preachers, troublemakers, statesmen, rich and poor, educated and uneducated—they became united in their desire for liberty, and they were willing to sacrifice much to be free.

This hands-on investigation of the Boston Tea Party actually begins with the seemingly satisfied colonists in America going about their daily lives with few complaints in the mid 1700s. Then a new king of England brought about some changes that made the colonists think twice about their relationship with the mother country. The exciting details of this period bring to life the people, their feelings and the consequent events that were the beginnings of the United States of America—"one nation, under God, indivisible, with liberty and justice for all." Teachers are provided with background information and meaningful activities that will give children an exciting glimpse into the birth of a nation. Children are able to experience firsthand the thrill and wonder of those times and events. Through active participation, children will begin to understand and empathize with the people who, through sacrifice and courage and an enthusiasm that could not be contained, made the United States of America happen.

It was a volatile time and feelings ran high on both sides of the conflict. So hold on to your hat as you lead your students into a world of discovery that will stir your patriotism and make you want to wave the flag!

Sincerely,

Mary Tucker

Mary Tucker

Boston Tea Party

Colonies in America

In 1760 America was a much different country than it is today. The population was only about 1½ million. (Today's population is about 200 times that number!) Half a million of the population were black slaves. Almost all these people lived in 13 colonies that covered a 1500-mile strip along the Atlantic Ocean: Massachusetts, New Hampshire, Connecticut, Rhode Island, New York, Pennsylvania, New Jersey, Delaware, Maryland, Virginia, North Carolina, South Carolina and Georgia.

Geography Challenge

Have students find the 13 original colonies on a current map; then compare and contrast them with one another. Which is the largest? The smallest? The farthest south? The farthest north?

Have them look in an atlas to find out more about these 13 states today. Which has the greatest population? The least?

Copy page 6 and hand it out to students. Have them write the name of each colony on the correct shape.

When students have completed the page, check the answers together as a class and have students correct any mistakes so they can use their pages to play the following game.

Who Am I? Colony Identification

Give two clues about one of the colonies. (Example: I am the most southern colony. Right above me is South Carolina. Who am I?) Have students raise their hands to name the colony you described. When the first one has been identified, give two clues about a second colony. Continue the game until all 13 colonies have been described and identified.

Historic Coins

Have students cooperate in taking to class new quarters featuring each of the 13 original colonies. Tell them to look at the quarters carefully. Discuss the symbols on the quarters. What do they symbolize? For more information, check out: www.usmint.gov/kids.

Connecticut:	Charter oak tree (The Connecticut Charter was hidden from the British in this tree.)
Delaware:	Caesar Rodney (signer of the Declaration of Independence)
Georgia:	Peach
Maryland:	Maryland State Capitol building
Massachusetts:	Minuteman soldier
New Hampshire:	Old Man of the Mountain (famous tourist site)
New Jersey:	Washington crossing the Delaware
New York:	Statue of Liberty
North Carolina:	Wright Brothers' "First Flight" airplane
Pennsylvania:	State Commonwealth statue from the top of the Capitol dome
Rhode Island:	Sailboat (Rhode Island is known an the "sailing capital" of the world.)
South Carolina:	State bird and tree
Virginia:	Jamestown (first English settlement in America) Living in the Colonies

Boston Tea Party

Name _____

Name the Colonies

Write the name of each American colony in its correct location.

Connecticut
Delaware
Georgia
Maryland
Massachusetts
New Hampshire
New Jersey
New York
North Carolina
Pennsylvania
Rhode Island
South Carolina
Virginia

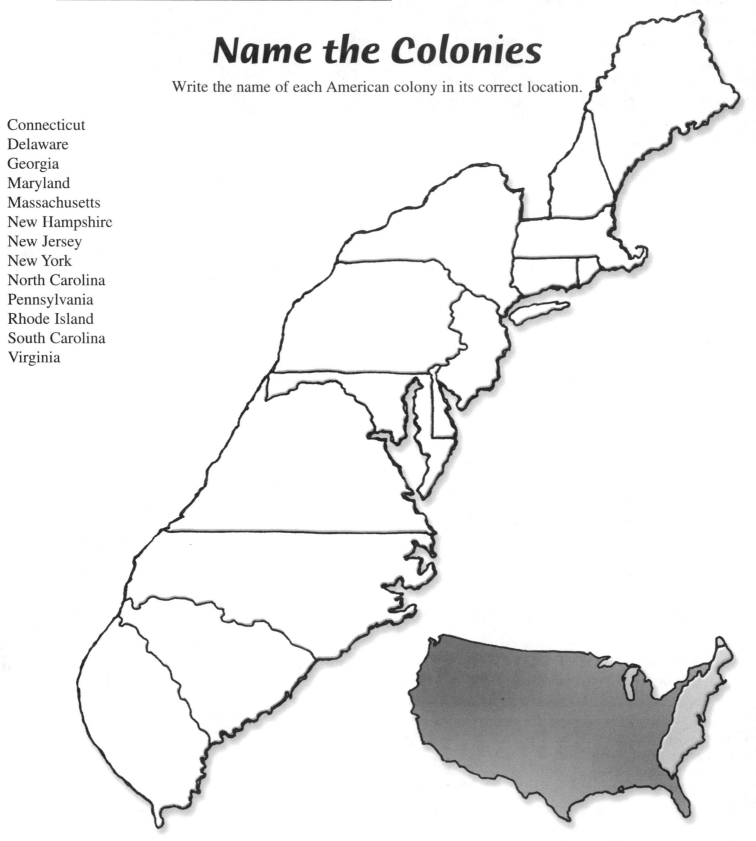

Boston Tea Party

Living in the Colonies

About $^9/_{10}$ of the people living in the colonies in the mid 1700s lived on small farms. Many lived in simple log cabins. A few in the southern colonies lived on huge farms called plantations. This was where most of the African American population lived as slaves. The farm families grew most of their own food and raised hogs, chickens and cows. They traded food with their neighbors and usually cooked the food in big iron pots hung over their fireplaces. It was a difficult life and everyone in the family had to work hard, even the children. Girls helped their mothers with cooking, sewing and making candles. Candlelight was usually the only light they had inside. Boys helped their fathers with the farm work–plowing, planting, harvesting, milking cows and so on. Most children didn't have a chance to go to school. Some larger towns had schools, but most children were taught a little reading and writing by their parents with the Bible as their textbook. Wealthy families were able to send their sons to private school or tutors, and a few of them went on to colleges such as Harvard and Yale.

Some people lived in towns where they worked at manufacturing, shopkeeping, medicine, printing, shipbuilding, fishing, law and foreign trade. Towns were small and separated by great distances though there were a few larger cities. Philadelphia, Pennsylvania, was the largest city with a population of 40,000; followed by New York with 20,000 and Boston with 16,000. Traveling near home was usually done by horse and carriage in town and by horse and wagon in the country. Rough roads that usually flooded and were sometimes washed away during heavy rains kept people from traveling far from home. Most travel far from home was done by water when possible.

Though children worked hard, they still found ways to have fun. They played ball, flew kites, spun tops and played marbles. They also jumped rope, blew soap bubbles, went swimming and fishing, rolled hoops, played with dolls and toy soldiers and pets and played leapfrog and hide-and-seek. Not only did children in the

American colonies play many of the same games children today play; they also sang some of the same songs such as "London Bridge Is Falling Down" and "Here We Go 'Round the Mulberry Bush."

Horse racing was a popular sport for the men, and men and women both liked to play card games and go horseback riding. And occasionally the whole family was able to enjoy a Punch and Judy puppet show or see a traveling circus that traveled from town to town. There were also fairs to go to with fun activities such as dancing and races to catch a greased pig.

Personal hygiene was different than it is today. Toothbrushes and toothpaste had not been invented yet in the 1700s. Many people never cleaned their teeth, but some people brushed their teeth with a twig and salt and water instead of toothpaste. They stripped the bark off the end of the twig and sometimes used a knife to cut the end into strips to make it softer. Children did not have to bathe almost every day as they do now. In fact, people thought it wasn't healthy to wash themselves too much. A once-a-week bath, or even less, was thought to be more than enough!

Colonial Fun and Games

Involve students in playing some of the quiet games colonial children played such as marbles and spinning tops as well as more active games such as leapfrog.

Then take students outside and let them find twigs to use to try brushing their teeth with salt and water. Make sure they peel the bark off the twigs first. Ask them why they think toothbrushes and toothpaste today do a better job.

Some larger towns had newspapers for people to read. *The Boston News-Letter* was the first newspaper in the colonies. By 1755 most of the colonies had at least one newspaper.

Everybody liked to have company. Visitors from other places brought news of what was happening there. Wealthy people who lived in big houses had plenty of guest rooms, and they could offer comfort to many overnight visitors. Poor families in the country, since they often lived in one-room cabins, made their overnight visitors welcome by moving over and giving them the warmest spot on the floor in front of the fireplace to sleep! When George Washington was a teenager, he did some work in the back country and stayed in the homes of poor families along the way. He usually slept on the floor with the family "like a parcel of dogs or cats" as he described it.

About three-fourths of the men living in the American colonies in the 1700s could read and write. Fewer women were able to do so since education was not considered important for them, and most slaves received no education. Paper was very expensive, so people experimented with other writing materials. Some used birch bark which peels easily off the tree and is almost white. A goose feather was often made into a pen by trimming the end of it into a point. Ink was usually made from the juice of berries or by boiling dark tree bark in water. The pointed end of the feather had to be dipped into the ink over and over again to write, so it was a slow process.

Writing Practice

Let students practice writing as the early colonists did. Provide each student with a large goose, duck or chicken feather. Use a knife to trim the ends of the feathers into points. (You may prefer to provide only a few trimmed feathers and let the children take turns writing with them.) Also provide non-permanent ink and heavy paper. Show students how to dip the feather quill into the ink; then let the excess ink drip off before writing with it on the paper. As students will discover, it was very difficult to write neatly without leaving a lot of ink blots on the paper.

If you decided to let them do this, provide adults' old shirts for smocks to keep the ink from splattering on their good clothes. You may also want to put newspapers on the table where they work to protect it (and maybe even on the floor under and around the table).

Boston Tea Party

Each colony elected officials who passed laws. There were also governors appointed by the British king to oversee things, but they rarely caused trouble, probably because they were paid by the American officials. Little by little, the colonists began thinking of themselves not as Englishmen, but as Americans, and they began having a different attitude about freedom, feeling they had a right to it. Besides, they thought, why did they need England? When the colonies were first settled, they had looked to British troops for protection, but Americans could take care of themselves now. They wanted to be free to make their own decisions, not ordered around by people who lived so far away they didn't know or care what was happening in the colonies.

Restrictions!

Parliament, the lawmaking branch of government for Great Britain, controlled the colonies' dealings with the rest of the world. The colonists could not sell many products, such as tobacco and cotton, to any country other than England. This did not make the colonists happy since they were offered better prices by other countries. Parliament also kept foreign products from being sold to the colonies, or they placed heavy taxes on them which made the colonists have to pay much more for them. Actually, most colonists were not terribly upset or inconvenienced by these restrictions. Since Parliament was far away, across the ocean, and the British Navy was unable to keep close watch on the whole Atlantic coast, it was fairly easy to smuggle goods in from forbidden countries. Smuggling was against the law, but most people in America were thankful to smugglers for their work because they brought in necessary goods at lower prices than they would have been if purchased according to British law.

Some smugglers anchored their ships in quiet places far away from the harbors where customs agents waited to collect fees from them. The smugglers sold their illegal cargo to colonists who took it to their homes and hid it. Other smugglers took their ships right up to the harbors where they bribed the customs agents to let them unload their goods without the usual fees.

The colonies were a good place to live where, unlike England, ordinary people who worked hard could prosper and make pleasant lives for themselves. At first the colonies accepted the idea that they belonged to Great Britain. They thought of themselves as British subjects who were creating a "New England" in America. They expected to have the rights that people back home in England had, and they accepted the idea that they owed allegiance to the king and obedience to the laws of Parliament. But there was one big difference in America and England–distance. The American colonies were weeks or even months away from their king and other leaders. Orders and laws might take six months to get to the colonies. So, of course, the colonies needed to be able to at least partly govern themselves.

Boston Tea Party

Name _____

Hidden Cargo

This smuggler's ship has five items hidden among the regular cargo.
Can you find them? Circle a bottle of wine, a box of tea, some cloth, a vase and a necklace.

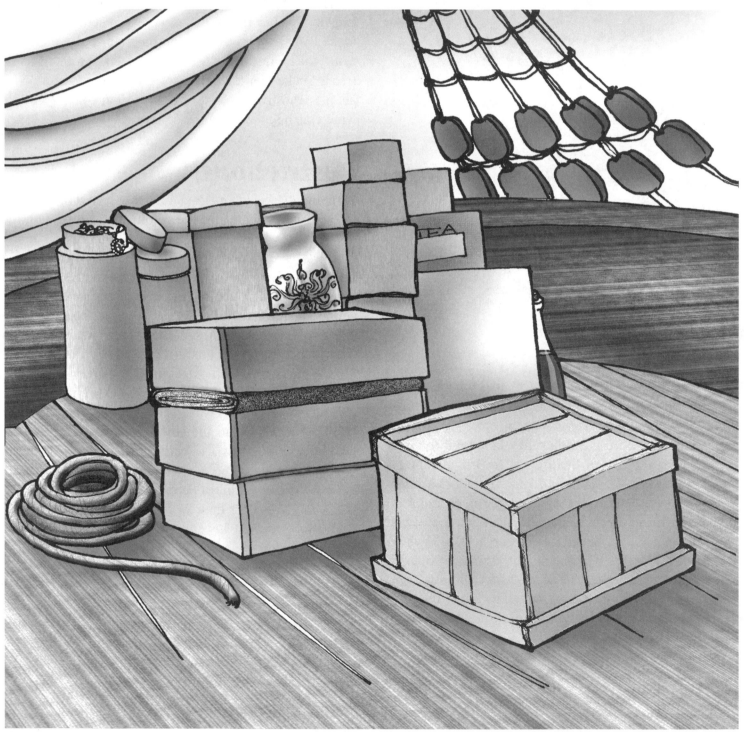

Boston Tea Party

Finding Smuggled Items

Reproduce page 10 for each student. Challenge them to discover the smuggled items hidden in the picture.

Making and Obeying Laws

Divide the class into two groups—a lawmaking group and a law-abiding group. Let the lawmaking group come up with three rules which the other group must obey. (Give the lawmaking group a clue that these rules need not be reasonable and can even be unpleasant.) Call on a confident member of the lawmaking team to read the new rules aloud in a brash, haughty manner.

Ask the law-abiding group how they feel about the rules. Do they like them? Are they good rules? Will they obey them? Is it okay for one group of students to make rules for them? Does this make them feel differently toward the students in the lawmaking group? What is the best way to settle this situation?

Repeat the procedure, switching the groups so both groups have a chance to create rules which their classmates must obey. Ask the new law-abiding group how they feel about someone else making rules for them now.

A Money-Making Land

Parliament might pass all the laws they chose for the American colonies, but it wasn't always easy to enforce the laws. How do you make people who live an ocean away do what you want? The only way was to send soldiers into each colony to see that the law was obeyed. But that was too expensive. England wanted to make money from the colonies, not spend more money on them. America was a fertile land with forests filled with wild animals and waters filled with fish. As long as the colonists kept buying English products and sending wheat, rice, fish, tobacco and furs to England, English investors were happy. After all, that's why British investors had sponsored and supported many settlers to the new world. Early explorers who went back from seeing America told amazing stories of the natural resources of the land and the wealth to be had there. In 1606 English merchants had sent men to found Jamestown, Virginia, the first permanent English settlement in the new world. By the end of the century, England was receiving shiploads of fish, iron, lumber, whale products and tobacco from America. Colonizing America had turned out to be a very smart investment. When profits began to fall because Americans were ignoring the laws, something had to be done!

Rich America Action Rhyme

Teach students the following action rhyme about the riches the English found in America.

Lumber from the forests,
(Stretch out arms like tree limbs and sway.)

Fish from the sea,
(Put hands together and move them like swimming fish.)

Animal furs and cotton to make clothes for me!
(Pretend to put on a coat.)

America is wonderful!
(Spread out arms to indicate a big area.)

America is grand!
(Spread out arms and twirl around.)

Riches everywhere you look,
(Shade eyes with hand and look around.)

Money in my hand!
(Hold out one open hand and slap it with the other.)

Boston Tea Party

A New King

It was just about the time that Americans began to resent the intrusion of England in their lives that a new king took over. King George III was only 22 years old. He had high morals (which certainly was not true of many kings) and was a devoted family man who had 15 children by the time he was 33. He was sometimes called "Farmer George" because of his interest in agriculture. He wasn't very intelligent. He was 11 years old before he could read and was once referred to by a British scholar as "a clod of a boy whom no one could teach."

He took a far greater part in governing his country than his father, George II, had done. In fact, George III thought his father had led England near to ruin. During his reign, Britain gained territories in Africa, Asia and Australia. He believed that God had given him the British Empire to rule, but he wasn't a very wise ruler. Once he made his mind up about something, it was almost impossible to change it. Some members of Parliament strongly opposed his treatment of the American colonists. One of his strongest opponents, William Pitt, collapsed as he was delivering a fiery attack on the British government's American policies in Parliament. But George III was so sure he was right, he stubbornly stuck to his ideas no matter how foolish they were. "I wish nothing but good," he said. "Therefore everyone who does not agree with me is a traitor and a scoundrel." He refused to listen to those who warned that he would not be able to enforce the laws he inflicted on the colonists in the face of armed American resistance.

A Royal Song

Ask students how they would like to be a king. Let them share their ideas about what that would be like. Younger students may enjoy making construction paper crowns and wearing them as they tell what they would do if they were king.

Then play a tape or CD of the song "I Just Can't Wait to Be King" from Disney's *The Lion King* movie. Many students will know this song, so encourage them to sing along.

Discussion

Ask students if they think a king always gets to do anything he wants. Explain that King George III of England was able to do most of what he wanted because he bribed some members of Parliament with money to go along with his ideas. The king's power also made it possible for him to influence lawmakers to go along with him on many issues. He gave government jobs to friends and people he knew would not oppose his wishes. If someone in an important position didn't go along with the king, he could have that person replaced with someone more willing to do what the king wanted. These were not unusual actions for a king in those days. Today, these ways of ruling are illegal in England and most other countries.

Ask students what advice they would give George III for being a good king. Have them consider if they had been king, what they would have done to improve relations between England and the American colonies.

Discuss the importance of wise advisors for any national leader, king or president. Ask students what kind of people they would want to advise them if they were king or president.

Boston Tea Party

The Stamp Act

King George III trusted Britain's Prime Minister, George Grenville, to make most of the decisions about the American colonies for him. Great Britain had recently won a war with France, the French and Indian War. It had cost Britain a lot of money. The national debt had nearly doubled, and the Prime Minister had to figure out how to save money. One way was to make the American colonists themselves pay for the army of British soldiers stationed in America. After all, the soldiers were there to protect the colonists, so why shouldn't they pay for them?

Mr. Grenville thought he could solve his problem with the Stamp Act. This was a direct tax on almost every paper or document used in the colonies: marriage certificates, college diplomas, bills of sale, wills, mortgages, newspapers and even playing cards. If a document did not have the official stamp on it, it was useless and the person who tried to use it would be fined! It was not one of the Prime Minister's best ideas. American colonists were furious about the Stamp Act. It wasn't the amount they had to pay that angered them; it was the idea that their elected officials had not been consulted or involved in the passing of the tax. Who did the Prime Minister of Great Britain think he was, ordering Americans around without even consulting them? "Taxation without representation!" became the cry of every colonist. They reasoned that if they could be taxed without their consent on the papers they used, they could be taxed on anything and everything! Americans suddenly felt their freedom had been taken away from them.

Classroom Stamps

Show students page 14 so they can see what some of the British stamps looked like. Then let them make their own to use in a classroom activity.

Materials
art paper
pencils
markers or crayons
gummed paper (or glue sticks)
envelopes
play money or pennies

Directions
1. Let students design and color their own stamps.
2. Have each student make six copies of his or her stamp on a sheet of gummed paper, or you may duplicate them on a copy machine. If gummed paper is not available, have each student cut out his or her stamps and put them in an envelope with a glue stick.
3. Assign each student something in the classroom to be in charge of such as paper, pencils, erasers, crayons, markers, pencil sharpener, tissues, etc.
4. Hand out classroom coins, pennies or play money to students. Whenever a student wants to use one of the items, he or she must buy a stamp from the student in charge of the item. (Want to use the pencil sharpener? That'll cost you a three-penny stamp!)

Discussion
Ask students how they would like it if this was the procedure in their lives outside school. What if they had to buy a stamp every time they wanted to eat a snack or get a drink, watch TV or use the computer, brush their teeth or turn on the light? Would they resent the person they have to pay and the person who made the rule? Why?

This is the Place to affix the STAMP.

We oppose the Stamp Act!

Boston Tea Party

British Stamps for America

Stamping on the Stamp Act

Representatives from nine of the American colonies met in New York City to officially condemn the Stamp Act. Others refused to buy any British products unless the Stamp Act was done away with. British goods piled up in warehouses because no one would buy them. Some colonists who called themselves Sons of Liberty bullied the people in charge of selling the stamps, sometimes throwing rocks through their windows to frighten them.

After about a year of the Americans' rebellion the Stamp Act was repealed. There just wasn't any way England could force people to obey it. The colonists were thrilled at their victory! They danced in the streets and lit bonfires. But while they were celebrating, they didn't realize that the British Parliament was passing another law that would restrict their freedom even more. The Declaratory Act said that Parliament had the power to make any law it chose for America. It could even end the little bit of self-government the colonists were enjoying in America.

Trying Out Self-Government

Let students experiment with self-government. Explain that they will elect four students to make rules for the class. They will also determine the punishment for not obeying the rules. Follow parliamentary procedure to conduct the meeting. Allow students to nominate candidates for class representatives. After several candidates have been nominated, ask if the class is ready for the nominating part of the meeting to be closed. If so, a student should raise his or her hand and say, "I move that nominations cease." Another student must raise a hand and second the motion. Then the class votes on it with raised hands.

Ask the candidates if they wish to accept or reject their nominations. Those who accept can then be voted on. Pass out slips of paper on which students may vote for four students to represent the class. Collect the ballots and count them as soon as possible. If possible, select two or three students to help with the counting. When all the votes have been counted, write the names of the four elected representatives on the board.

Set aside a time to meet with these class representatives. Explain to them that their duty will be to come up with fair rules and punishments for their class. Remind them that they need to find out what their classmates want before they come to any decisions.

After the representatives have decided on some rules, have them present their decisions to the class. Then ask students how they feel about the rules. Do they like them? Are they good rules? Will they obey them? Were their opinions asked? Do they feel differently about these rules than they did about the rules forced on them by the lawmaking group earlier in this study? What is the difference?

Boycott

The Stamp Act hadn't worked well, but the British Parliament didn't give up on getting money out of the Americans. The next year they passed the Townshend Act which made Americans pay for many English goods that came into American ports. Suddenly, the colonists had to pay even higher prices for paper, paint, glass, lead, cloth and tea. Once again, the colonists refused to pay. Instead, they began a boycott; they just quit using those products.

Some American women who called themselves Daughters of Liberty refused to marry men who used English products. Housewives started serving their husbands coffee instead of tea. The coffee was smuggled in from another country. A few people still drank tea, but it wasn't English tea. It was smuggled in from other countries. Women stopped using English cloth to make their clothes. They learned how to spin their own wool and cotton so they didn't have to rely on British materials. This was a real sacrifice for them since the finest fabrics and clothing styles came from England. Of course, country women, especially those with less money, had been spinning their own yarn and weaving it into cloth for some time. Perhaps it was these country women who taught their "city sisters" to spin and weave. Spinning schools were set up in churches, and women got together for all-day spinning bees to make their own cloth. This cloth was called homespun because they spun it themselves. It was much coarser than the machine-spun cloth they were used to, but Americans wore their homespun proudly as a symbol of their desire for freedom.

Sheep's wool was spun into yarn on spinning wheels of various kinds. First the wool had to be washed and dried, then "teased." To do this a woman held a clump of wool in one hand and gently loosened the fibers with the other hand. This made the wool open and fluffy so it was easier to spin. Some women had large spinning wheels while those with less money had to spin their wool by hand, winding it on a hooked stick. Either way, spinning was a time-consuming task that took a lot of patience. Having a friend to talk to while spinning made the work a lot more enjoyable.

Spinning & Weaving

Spinning

Materials
bundle of natural sheep's wool (available at craft stores)
empty thread spools

Directions
1. Give each student a small amount of the wool.
2. Show students how to gently but firmly pull a small quantity of tangled fibers from the bundle. Then they should gently rub the fibers between their fingers to form a rough length of yarn and begin wrapping the the yarn around the spool.
3. When they're done with the first length of yarn, they should repeat the process, attaching the new length to the one already on the spool by weaving the two together as smoothly as possible.

16

Boston Tea Party

Weaving

To make fabric, students will need to weave yarn. Provide yarn for them to use since they won't have time to spin wool into enough yarn in the time available.

Materials
approximately 8½ feet of yarn for each student
(preferably of two different colors)
cardboard
ruler
pen or pencil
scissors
masking tape
large darning needle (or a craft stick)

Directions
1. Cut a 7" x 5" rectangle out of the cardboard.
2. Draw a line ¼" from each of the shorter edges.
3. Draw a row of angled lines on each edge and cut along them to make a notched edge as shown.
4. Tape one end of the yarn on the back of the cardboard loom near the bottom left-hand notch.
5. Wind the yarn around the loom from top to bottom, hooking it in the notches. (Don't let the yarn be too loose; wind it fairly tightly.)
6. Tape down the other loose end of the yarn on the back of the loom and cut off extra yarn.
7. Thread the second color of yarn through the darning needle or tie it to the craft stick. Pull the yarn from left to right under and over the yarn already on the loom. When that line is done, do another line from right to left, over and under.
8. Continue weaving the yarn until you have a piece of fabric.
9. When you're done weaving, tie the end pieces of yarn and carefully remove the piece of fabric from the loom.

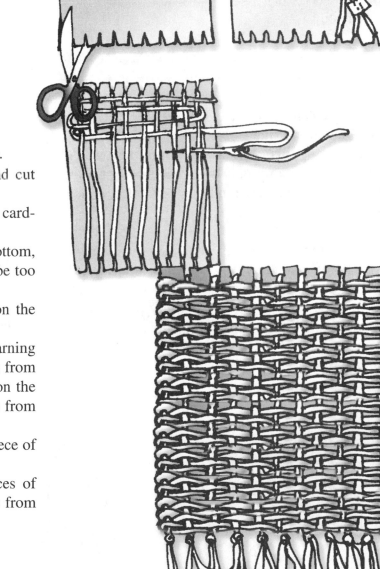

Boston Tea Party

Redcoats

The Sons of Liberty mistreated and even tortured those who didn't cooperate and bought British goods. When a crowd of angry colonists beat up English custom agents, the British government decided they'd had enough. Those rebellious colonists needed to be taught a lesson. British warships were sent to Boston and hundreds of Redcoats, British soldiers, marched through town with loaded guns. The colonists knew the soldiers were there to stay when they pitched their tents in the center of the city.

The people of Boston didn't like having the Redcoats everywhere in their town, especially since they were there to enforce unjust laws. After all, the colonies had their own army, called a militia. The soldiers were only part time, but several times a year they drilled to keep up their military skills. And if war came they would serve full-time, at least for a few weeks or months. Nobody made them be in the militia; they did it of their own free will to help America.

The Redcoats were entirely different. Being a common soldier for the British army was a job few men wanted. No one enlisted unless he had to. Many of the Redcoats were criminals who had joined the army to avoid the death penalty. Army life was horrible. The Redcoat uniform was a bright red overcoat with metal buttons and tight white pants. Two belts to hold the soldier's bayonet and bullet box crisscrossed his chest in an X.

Dressin' Like a Redcoat

Let students make their own red coats like the British soldiers.

Materials
large paper grocery bag for each student
white crepe paper or adding machine tape
clear tape
red crayons or paint
scissors
silver wrapping paper or foil
glue

Directions
1. Show children how to cut the paper bag down the middle from the top to the flat bottom. Then cut out a circle in the flat bottom for a neck hole. (Make sure the hole is large enough so it doesn't scratch the child's neck.) Cut armholes in the sides of the bag. If possible, have some adults ready to help younger children with the cutting.
2. Let students use crayons or paint to color the bags red all over.
3. Show students how to cut circles from the silver paper or foil and glue them down the front of the coat for metal buttons.
4. Have each student put on his or her red coat. Then cut strips from white crepe paper or adding machine tape and place them over the coat in a big X. If you make each strip into a big loop taped together at the ends, the two can be put over the student's head and easily slipped on or off.

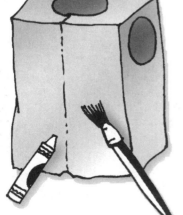

Boston Tea Party

The colonists harassed the Redcoats by throwing garbage at them or pushing them down from the back, then running away. Loud arguments, shouting and even fistfights between the British soldiers and the American colonists happened almost every day in Boston. Everybody knew that something even worse would happen sooner or later.

Soldiers had to carry heavy gear and food as they marched. For all of their hard work, they earned about two cents a day! They often tried to find other jobs during their off-duty hours to make extra money. This made the citizens of Boston even angrier. "Those Lobsterbacks are taking the jobs we need!" they complained. The British soldiers ridiculed the colonists, and the colonists taunted the soldiers and called them names. The Redcoats made fun of the American colonists by singing "Yankee Doodle" about them. The song described the colonists as dishonest, unfair and foolish.

Singing About Freedom

Have students sing "Yankee Doodle" as they march around the room wearing their red coats. Then explain that later on the Americans turned the song back on the British and sang it about them.

Teach students new words to this old song to help them remember what the American colonists wanted from England. Have them take off their British uniforms, then sing this version of the song.

To the tune of "Yankee Doodle"

Long ago in history before we were a nation,
Some brave men said, "We must be free!" America's foundation.

Chorus

Freedom is the thing we want; liberty forever!
We will fight until we win. We won't give up—no, never!

Discussion
Discuss the words of the song. Ask students to share their ideas about what true freedom is. Explain that when we say freedom is America's foundation, we're saying that freedom is what the nation is built on. Then explain that *liberty* is another word for *freedom*.

Ask students to think how they would have felt if they had lived in America when the King of England was in charge. Would they have been willing to fight for freedom from British rule? Point out that many colonists gave up far more than tea or English cloth. Some had their homes and possessions taken away; others gave their lives for the cause of freedom.

The Boston Massacre

It wasn't long before the harsh feelings between the American colonists and the British soldiers boiled over into a serious clash. Hugh White, a private in the British army, was standing guard on a Boston street one night when he got into an argument with a teenager who lived in Boston. When the soldier hit the colonist with the end of his gun, the boy ran off, returning a little later with a group of friends. They began calling Private White ugly names, and as they shouted at him a crowd gathered. The crowd grew larger and they began shouting "Kill the soldier!" as they threw stone-filled snowballs at him. Terrified, the British Redcoat called for help. Other soldiers rushed out to help him fight off the angry crowd. They poked their bayonet-tipped guns at the troublemakers, but did not dare shoot at them. Any soldier who shot at someone without receiving an order to do so could be punished by hanging. Then a big man in the crowd hit one of the soldiers with a club and hit another one in the head, knocking him down. The Redcoats, in fear for their lives, began shooting into the crowd. Soon five Americans lay dead in the snowy street.

The British soldiers were charged with murder and put in jail. John Adams, who later became the second President of the United States, defended them at their trial. Adams wanted freedom from England and didn't like having British soldiers in his town, but he believed the accused men deserved a fair trial. The soldiers were found innocent of murder and freed. But the memory of the shooting still made many people very angry. Paul Revere, an engraver and silversmith, kept resentment and anger toward the British alive with an engraving he made of the "Bloody Massacre," as he called it. The scene he drew showed British soldiers gleefully shooting down innocent, unarmed, peaceful citizens at their captain's command. For years, Paul Revere's engraving hung in Americans' homes and they accepted his version of the event.

Discussion

Who do you think was at fault in the Boston Massacre? Why did the crowd get so excited? Would you have been scared if you had been one of the British soldiers? Do you think the Redcoats were guilty or innocent of murder?

What happens when people make fun of others and say hateful things to tease them or make them angry? What can you do to be a peacemaker in this kind of situation? How can you live at peace with others even when they don't want to?

A Song About Peace

Teach students this song to help them think about how to live in harmony with others.

To the tune of "Row, Row, Row Your Boat"

If you want to live peacefully each day,
Be very kind to everyone
And careful what you say.

Boston Tea Party

Engraving Activity

Let students try this simplified form of engraving a picture.

Materials

heavy-duty aluminum foil
thick sheet of cardboard
masking tape
pencil with a dull point
some black paint
paintbrush
rag

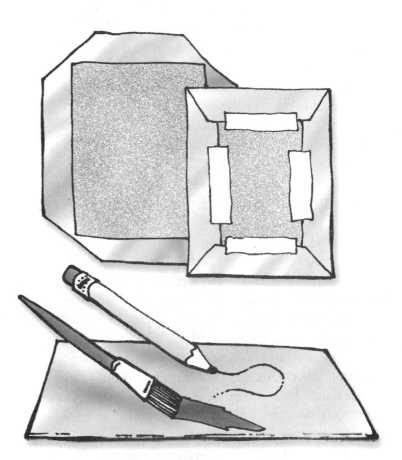

Directions

1. Have each student cover one side of the cardboard with aluminum foil, folding over the edges and securing them with masking tape on the back.
2. Show them how to use the dull-tipped pencil to impress a design or scene in the foil. (Warn them not to press too hard or they might tear the foil.) Have them make a design or scene based on the events they are studying (an early flag of the 13 colonies, a Redcoat, a stamp, British ships in Boston Harbor, etc.).
3. When the engraving is done, have the student brush a light coating of black paint over it; then lightly wipe most of the paint off with a rag. The black paint will remain in the engraved lines, causing the design or scene to stand out.
4. Display the engravings on a classroom bulletin board or wall.

Explain that Paul Revere's engravings were a little different. He engraved a scene, then used it as a pattern from which to print paper copies of the scene.

Paul Revere later helped organize the Boston Tea Party and acted as one of the Mohawks in that event.

Boston Tea Party

More Trouble

After the Boston Massacre the British tried to calm down things in Boston. The Redcoats were sent from town to stay in Castle William, a fortress on an island in Boston Harbor. Parliament repealed the Townshend Act, but the tax on tea remained in force. This was to show Americans that Parliament had the right to tax the colonies. The American boycott on British goods also ended, but the colonists still refused to buy tea. Neither side was willing to give in, but there was no trouble for a while.

Then England's new prime minister, Lord North, made a dangerous error. Lord North didn't really know much about the Americans. He certainly didn't want war between England and the American colonies. He was just trying to help his countrymen. The East India Company was a large company that imported tea into Great Britain and sold it to London merchants. Those London merchants then sold the tea to American merchants to sell in the colonies. But since the American colonists were still refusing to buy tea from England, the East India Company was unable to sell it to the London merchants, and it began piling up in their warehouses. The East India Company was losing so much money, it was in danger of going out of business! So Lord North decided to do something to help. He would allow the East India Company to sell their tea directly to the Americans. This would mean that the Americans would be able to buy tea at a much lower price than before, so they wouldn't be forced to buy smuggled tea or drink coffee instead. Lord North thought this would make the Americans forget about the tax on tea and everyone would be happy.

Lord North was wrong. American colonists saw this move as an attempt to trick them into giving in to the British and ending their boycott. If that happened, the British would think they could do anything they wanted to the colonists. Americans resisted Lord North's plan. Angry crowds waited on city docks to turn away British ships carrying tea, and would not allow them to unload their shipments.

Tea: The Favorite Drink

The boycott on tea hadn't been easy on the American colonists, but they had stuck to it. Tea was the favorite drink in the colonies, but freedom was more important! And now the English were trying to use tea to fool the colonists into giving in and accepting that Parliament knew what was best for them. But they would rather never drink tea again than to give up their principles!

Tea was the national drink of England, but it actually came to America a couple of years before the English discovered it. A Dutch trader took tea to New Amsterdam in 1650. Later when the English took over New Amsterdam and renamed it New York, they found that the people there drank more tea than in all of England!

Tea came from ancient China thousands of years ago and was taken to Japan by a Buddhist priest who is known as the Father of Tea in Japan. Europeans began hearing about tea from caravan leaders who could give few details about it. One thought the tea leaves should

be boiled, salted, buttered and eaten! But the people of Europe soon discovered the right way to use tea leaves when Dutch ships began taking it from the Orient.

English colonists in Boston did not become aware of tea until 1670, and it was not available for sale until 1690. It soon became a favorite drink, especially of colonial women. But tea was more than a drink. It was a celebration, a reason for taking a break from work to relax and visit with friends and family, and a tradition. Cakes, muffins and other sweet treats were often served with afternoon tea. Even in the poorest homes, tea time included bread and butter.

Trevelyan, an English historian said about tea in America: "The . . . most easily prepared of beverages, it was drunk in the backwoods of America . . . . In more settled districts, the quantity absorbed on all occasions of ceremony is incredible . . . ." Tea played an important part not only in the everyday life of colonial America, but also in the American Revolution.

During the colonial boycott on English tea, Americans began drinking more coffee and though tea is a popular drink today, it has never regained the popularity it had before the Boston Tea Party. However, when the new American nation began direct trade with China after the War of Independence, many men made fortunes. The first three millionaires in America all made their fortunes in the China trade.

Though Americans can't claim to have invented tea, they have done some original things with it. At the St. Louis World's Fair in 1904, a tea plantation owner had planned to give away free samples of hot tea to fair visitors. However, the weather was so hot no one was interested in a hot drink. He dumped a load of ice into the hot tea and served the first "iced tea." It was one of the most popular things at the fair.

Four years later a New York tea merchant carefully wrapped each tea sample he delivered to restaurants, hoping they would buy his tea. When he discovered that the restaurants were brewing the tea samples in their wrappings to avoid the mess of tea leaves, tea bags were born.

Today there are many different kinds of tea from all over the world, including herbal teas and green tea, and tea is once again gaining in popularity.

Teatime

Provide a variety of teas for children to look at, smell and taste. Label each kind. Include both tea leaves and tea bags. Have both hot tea and iced tea for them to taste. Give older students a copy of the questionnaire on page 24 to fill out after their tea examinations. After this teatime, ask students to share their feelings about tea. Chart their likes and dislikes to discover class preferences.

Plan an afternoon teatime for the class. Brew tea and pour it from a teapot into Styrofoam™ cups for the children. Offer sugar or honey for their tea, and provide cookies.

Boston Tea Party

Name _____

Tea Questionnaire

As you examine and taste the teas your teacher has provided, answer the following questions:

1. Which tea smells the best? _____

2. Which tea tastes the best? _____

3. Which do you like better–hot tea or iced tea? _____

4. Which do you think is easier to use–loose tea leaves or tea bags? Explain why. _____

_____

5. Which do you like best?   _____ tea with sugar   _____ tea with honey   _____ tea with no sweetener

6. Does anyone in your family drink tea often? If so, who? _____

_____

7. Which do you like better to smell first thing in the morning–hot coffee or hot tea? _____

Boston Tea Party

A Saltwater Tea Party

On December 16, 1773, in the dark of night, a group of colonial men in Boston dressed as Mohawk Indians took matters into their own hands. Each man's face was painted red or blackened with chimney soot; he had a blanket wrapped around his body, and he carried an axe. The phony Indians marched quietly two by two to the wharf where three British tea ships were anchored. A group of 25 volunteers, many of them Sons of Liberty, were already standing guard with loaded guns to keep the ships' cargo from being brought ashore. The disguised colonists climbed aboard the ships and took the chests of tea up onto the deck. The ships' crews stood aside and watched, not willing to fight and possibly get injured to save the loads of tea. By the light of the moon the Mohawks broke open the tea chests and threw the tea into the water, making what they called "saltwater tea."

"We used no more words than were absolutely necessary," said Joshua Wyeth, one of the participants. "I never worked harder in my life." A large crowd of colonists watched in almost complete silence. Two British warships anchored in the harbor reminded everyone of the need to get the job done quietly without attracting unwanted attention. No one did anything to stop the phony Indians. It was all over in less than three hours. The only injury was accidental when one of the participants, John Crane, was knocked down by a piece of hoisting equipment. He was not killed, but remained unconscious for a while.

When the tea party was over, each participant had to open his coat to show that he had not stolen any tea. One man was punished when it was discovered that he had filled his coat and shoes with tea leaves. The ships' decks were swept clean and everything was put back in place. Nothing on the ships was damaged except for the tea chests.

The Mohawks marched silently down the street until they were too far away for anyone on the British warships to hear them. Then everyone began laughing and marching proudly with a fife playing "Yankee Doodle."

As the men returned home from the "party" to wash their faces and get rid of their disguises, tea floated on the water as far as could be seen. The next day American colonists were singing a new song:

> Rally, Mohawks! Bring out your axes.
> Let's tell King George we'll pay no taxes
> On his foreign tea!

Paul Revere was chosen to ride to New York and Philadelphia to carry news of the destruction of the tea. Those American colonists, like those in Boston, considered the tea party a great victory when they heard about it. However when word reached England, King George was not amused. "The colonies must either submit or triumph," he wrote to Lord North. The king should have figured out by then that the Americans were never going to submit!

Tea Party Song

Duplicate the song on page 28, and have students sing it together to celebrate the Boston Tea Party.

Boston Tea Party

Tea Party Pantomime

Students will enjoy acting out the Boston Tea Party. Let them disguise themselves as Indians as the original tea partiers did.

Materials

makeup or Halloween face paints
large bath towels (which may be used as blankets)
colored construction paper
cardboard
string
scissors
glue

Directions

1. Let students use makeup or face paint to color their faces. You may want to let them work in pairs, making up one another's faces.
2. Show students how to cut feather shapes from various colors of construction paper.
3. Have students cut out construction paper headbands and glue the paper feathers to them. They'll need to attach string to the ends of the headbands to tie them on their heads.
4. Let students cut tomahawks from construction paper.
5. Have each student wrap a large towel around himself or herself to complete the Indian disguise.
6. Arrange the front or back of the room to be an imaginary ship. For realism, stack empty cardboard boxes for students to tear open.
7. Line students up and remind them that the tea party is to be silent. They don't want the British to hear them! Have them march to the imaginary ship and break open the boxes, pretending to dump the contents into the water.
8. When all the tea has been dumped, have students quietly line up and march around the room to the tune of "Yankee Doodle."

Patriot's Cheer

Ask students to give their definitions of *patriotism*. Explain that a patriot is a person who loves his or her country and is loyal to it. Go over the list of patriots on page 31, discussing what they did for their country. The American colonists loved America and were loyal to it rather than to England. Have students pretend they are American colonists as they shout this cheer for their country.

What is the greatest land anywhere today?
A-M-E-R-I-C-A!
Where can you be free to live in your own way?
A-M-E-R-I-C-A!
What is the best place to learn and grow and play?
A-M-E-R-I-C-A!
America! America! Our home–America!
Yea! Yea! Yea!

Discussion

Why do you think the colonists disguised themselves as Indians to get rid of the tea? Why do you think the tea party participants were so careful not to harm anything but the tea chests on the British ships and not take any of the tea home with them?

Boston Tea Party

Punishment from Parliament

The British were angry at what the Americans had done in Boston. Parliament quickly went to work and passed three "Intolerable Acts" meant to punish the colony of Massachusetts especially. The Massachusettts Government Act ended self-government for that colony. The Quartering Act said that the British army could take over private buildings. That meant a colonist's home could be taken over as a place for Redcoats to sleep! The Boston Port Act closed Boston Harbor until all the tea that had been destroyed was paid for. The people of Boston couldn't even send a ferry across their own harbor. Fishermen couldn't take their boats out fishing. No food could be shipped in. What would happen to the people with no food or supplies coming in? It was a harsh punishment that showed England's strength. And in the spring, thousands of British soldiers arrived in Boston to enforce the new laws.

But the Americans would not be bullied by the British. Every colony did what it could to help the people of Massachusetts. Cattle, sheep, hogs, fish and grain were shipped to nearby ports, then taken by wagon to Boston. The Americans would stick together.

In every colony part-time soldiers volunteered to be minutemen, promising to be ready for action at a minute's notice. Smugglers took gunpowder from the West Indies. Bands of undercover agents led by men like Paul Revere secretly stole British guns, even cannons, and ruined British supplies and materials. America was preparing for war with England!

Remembering a Special Time

Duplicate page 29 for students to look at and color. After they count the 13 stripes on the flag, can they say what the stripes stand for? Remind them that every time we pledge allegiance to the American flag, we are also remembering those first 13 American colonies, one for every stripe on the flag. The 50 stars on the flag remind us how those original 13 colonies have grown to become 50 United States.

The middle of the 1700s was a special time in America's history. We wouldn't be here today living in a free land where we can do almost anything we want if it hadn't been for those colonists who were willing to work hard and sacrifice for what they believed in. Duplicate page 30 for each student to complete as a review of what they have learned about life in America before the colonies became a nation.

Then duplicate the song on page 28 and have students sing it together to review and celebrate the Boston Tea Party, that wonderful event that showed the King of England and the whole world that Americans wanted to be free and nothing was going to stop them!

A Tea Party Tune

To the tune of "This Old Man"

England thinks they'll fool us.
We'll buy tea and never fuss,
So let's go and dump it all into the sea.
We'll call it saltwater tea!

Quietly, in disguise,
We'll cut King George down to size
When we dump his shipments all into the sea.
Hope he likes saltwater tea.

All around, everywhere,
The smell of tea leaves fills the air.
It's a lovely smell, at least it is to me.
Yes, I love saltwater tea!

Now the job is all done;
We worked hard, but it was fun.
And we showed the world our longing to be free
When we made saltwater tea.

Sing this song often until children can sing it by heart. Younger children will enjoy acting out the song as they sing it. Discuss the words to make sure students understand exactly what they mean. For example, do they understand what it means to "cut King George down to size"?

If time permits, work together as a class to write additional verses to sing.

The American Flag Today

Name _____

Count the number of stripes on the flag. What do they stand for? Count the number of stars on the flag. What do they stand for? Now follow the directions to color the flag.

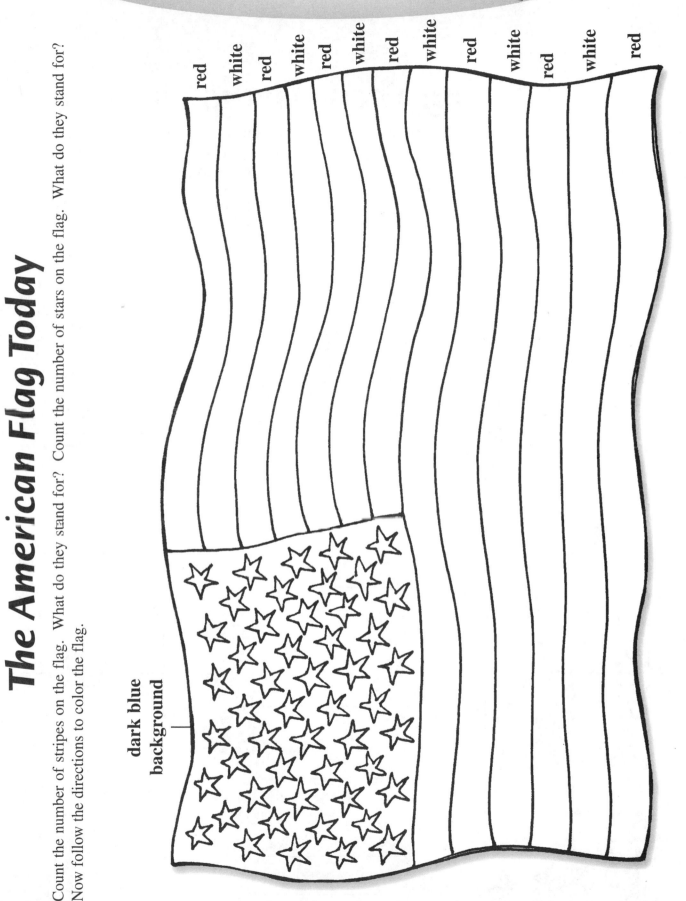

red white red white red white red white red white red white red

dark blue background

Name _____

Living Then—Living Now

Life in colonial America was very different in many ways than it is today. The items people used for important, everyday tasks were not nearly as helpful as the items we use today. Write next to each picture below the name of the item and what it was used for. Then draw a picture to the right of it to show what we use today in place of it.

Famous American Patriots

Colonial patriots loved America and were loyal to it. Many of them worked hard, put their lives in danger and sacrificed much for America's freedom. Read about and discuss the patriotism of the following men. Challenge older students to do further research to discover additional information about patriots of their choice. Younger students will enjoy acting out some of the events mentioned such as the signing of the Declaration of Independence, hiding from the British, riding to New York to tell of the Boston Tea Party, etc.

John Adams (1735-1826)
- Boston lawyer who wrote resolutions of protest against Britain's Stamp Act
- Defended Redcoats involved in the Boston Massacre in court
- Signer of the Declaration of Independence (Thomas Jefferson gave him credit for getting it approved by Congress.)
- George Washington's Vice President
- Second American President

Samuel Adams (1722-1803)
- Radical patriot and political agitator who organized colonial opposition against British laws
- Called "The Man of the Revolution" by Thomas Jefferson

John Crane (1744-1805)
- Fought in the French and Indian War at age 15
- One of Boston's Sons of Liberty
- Participant in the Boston Tea Party (While he was helping to get tea chests on deck, a hoist fell on him, knocking him unconscious. His friends thought he was dead, but he later revived.)
- Continental officer in the Revolutionary War

Benjamin Franklin (1706-1790)
- Editor of *Poor Richard's Almanack* (practical advice and proverbs still quoted today)
- Owned a newspaper, established a circulating library and Philadelphia's first fire company
- Postmaster General of the Colonies
- Colonial agent/ambassador in England, helped secure repeal of the Stamp Act
- Helped draft the Declaration of Independence and was one of its signers
- Represented America in France

John Hart (1711-1779)
- New Jersey patriot, farmer, politician
- Member of Continental Congress
- Signer of the Declaration of Independence
- The British destroyed his farm and livestock and he, at age 70, and his wife hid in the woods for several months to avoid capture. His wife died as a result.

John Hancock (1737-1793)
- Millionaire patriot who led the town committee to investigate the Boston Massacre
- Member (and President for two years) of the Continental Congress
- First signer of the Declaration of Independence (with the largest signature)

Patrick Henry (1736-1799)
- Patriotic speaker, statesman, lawyer from Virginia
- Urged armed resistance to the British and said, "Give me liberty, or give me death!"
- Colonel of the first Virginia army regiment
- Governor of Virginia after the war

Thomas Jefferson (1743-1826)
- Virginia statesman, lawyer, diplomat, scientist, architect, farmer
- Wrote the Declaration of Independence
- Member of the Continental Congress
- Third American President

Israel Putnam (1718-1790)
- Connecticut farmer, soldier and member of the Sons of Liberty
- When the British closed Boston Harbor as punishment for the Boston Tea Party, he drove a herd of 125 sheep into town to feed the hungry people.
- Colonel in the Revolutionary War

Boston Tea Party

Paul Revere (1735-1818)

- Patriot, craftsman (silversmith and engraver), courier (messenger)
- Helped organize and carry out the Boston Tea Party, then rode to New York to tell people there about it
- His engraved picture of the Boston Massacre helped keep colonists angry at the British.
- Printed the first Continental currency
- Directed the manufacturing of gunpowder for American forces in the war

Caesar Rodney (1728-1784)

- Patriot, colonel then brigadier general in the Delaware militia
- Signer of the Declaration of Independence

George Washington (1732-1799)

- Virginia statesman, farmer
- Commander-in-Chief of the Continental Army
- First American President
- Called "The Father of His Country"

Fascinating Facts About Colonial America

In 1763 the British government issued a royal proclamation that colonial settlement was forbidden between the Appalachian Mountains and the Mississippi River. That whole area was declared a reservation for Indians.

The 1700s have been called the Age of Enlightenment in history. Why? Because people began wanting to know about the world they lived in. They began asking questions. The colonists in America were asking questions about freedom.

America's 13 colonies covered an area of about 250,000 square miles, about three times the size of England.

Male colonists often cut their hair very short to avoid head lice, and then wore wigs made of goat, horse or human hair.

The only people in the colonies who could vote were men who owned property.

In 1760 the average colonist lived to be 40 years old.

Since there were few trained doctors in the American colonies in the mid 1700s, people came up with their own strange remedies. A woman giving birth to a child was supposed to drink cow's milk with ants' eggs and the hair of a young girl mixed into it!

If the fire in the fireplace of a colonial home went out, one of the children in the family took the "fire pan" to a neighbor's house to borrow some fire (burning embers from the neighbor's fire).

British soldiers wore red coats because in battle they marched in tight lines. When a soldier was shot, his red coat made it hard for others to know that he was bleeding. This kept the enemy from knowing the line had been weakened, and it helped stop the other British soldiers from getting scared and running away!

The British soldier's gun, called a musket, weighed about 14 pounds.

TLC10302 Copyright © Teaching & Learning Company, Carthage, IL 62321-0010